iPlayMusic, Inc.

For more information about iPlayMusic, Inc., please email us at info@iplaymusic.com.

www.iPlayMusic.com

T0087376

Co-authors: Quincy Carroll and Noel Rabinowitz
Childrens illustrations: Elizabeth Ann Cannom
Cover and book design: Chris Canote
Puppetry: Kamela Portuges and Images in Motion
Instructional illustrations: Mike Biegel
Graphic design: Karyn Nelson Designs
Editing: N.T. Raymond, Quincy Carroll, and Noel Rabinowitz
Consulting Editor: Rich Winter
Coloring illustration: Jennie Smith
Additional story development: Jennifer Carroll
Photography: Luke O'Byrne

Copyright © 2007 by iPlayMusic, Inc.
This book Published 2007 by Amsco Publications,
A Division of Music Sales Corporation, New York

Order No. IP10024
ISBN-10: 0-9760487-6-0
ISBN-13: 978-0-9760487-6-3

Exclusive Distributors:
Music Sales Corporation
257 Park Avenue South, New York, NY 10010 USA
Music Sales Limited
14-15 Berners Street, London W1T 3LJ England
Music Sales Pty. Limited
120 Rothschild Street, Rosebery, Sydney, NSW 2018, Australia

Printed in the United States of America by
Vicks Lithograph and Printing Corporation

Table of Contents

STORIES AND SONGS

BEGINNER GUITAR LESSONS: BASICS

iPlayMusic®

Play Music Together
STORIES AND SONGS

It's a beautiful day.
Capo is happy...
...and he knows it.

There's a
happy cool breeze
whistling through the trees.

The big pretty shells make the sound of the seas.

The sun moves through the sky with rhythm and ease.

Capo plays drums on coconut shells...

...and cheerful birds sing in the sky.

Chirp!

Chirp!

5

If You're Happy and You Know It

If you're happy and you know it,
clap your hands.

If you're happy and you know it,
clap your hands.

If you're happy and you know it
and you really want to show it...

If you're happy and you know it, clap your hands.

If you're happy and you know it, stomp your feet.

If you're happy and you know it, stomp your feet.

If you're happy and you know it
and you really want to show it...

If you're happy and you know it, stomp your feet.

If you're happy and you know it, shout "hooray!"

If you're happy and you know it, shout "hooray!"

If you're happy and you know it
and you really want to show it...

If you're happy and you know it, shout "hooray!"

HOORAY!

If you're happy and you know it, do all three.

If you're happy and you know it, do all three.

If you're happy and you know it
and you really want to show it...

If you're happy and you know it, do all three.

The little red car goes

Vroom
Vroom
Vroom!

And the kitty cat puppet goes

Meow
Meow
Meow.

The planes in the sky go

ZOOM
ZOOM
ZOOM.

And the wheels on the bus go ... how?

The Wheels on the Bus

The wheels on the bus go round and round,
round and round, round and round.
The wheels on the bus go round and round,
all through the town.

The wipers on the bus go
swish, swish, swish,
swish, swish, swish,
swish, swish, swish.
The wipers on the bus go
swish, swish, swish,
all through the town.

The horn on the bus goes
beep, beep, beep,
beep, beep, beep,
beep, beep, beep.
The horn on the bus goes
beep, beep, beep,
all through the town.

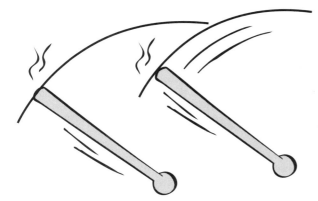

The money on the bus goes clink, clink, clink,
clink, clink, clink, clink, clink, clink.
The money on the bus goes clink, clink, clink,
all through the town.

The babies on the bus go
wah, wah, wah,
wah, wah, wah,
wah, wah, wah.
The babies on the bus go
wah, wah, wah,
all through the town.

The mommy on the bus goes
shh, shh, shh,
shh, shh, shh,
shh, shh, shh.
The mommy on the bus goes
shh, shh, shh,
all through the town.

Some people like to
play harp.

And some people like
to rock out.

Some people like the
ballet.

And some people just
twist and shout.

But everyone loves a
good song.

And everyone loves
to hold hands.

So, let's hold hands and sing this
song with Capo and his friends.

He's Got the Whole World in His Hands

He's got the whole world in His hands.

He's got the whole world in His hands.

He's got the whole world in His hands.

He's got the whole world in His hands.

He's got the wind and the rain in His hands.
He's got the wind and the rain in His hands.
He's got the wind and the rain in His hands.
He's got the whole world in His hands.

He's got the little bitty baby in His hands.
He's got the little bitty baby in His hands.
He's got the little bitty baby in His hands.
He's got the whole world in His hands.

He's got the whole world in His hands.
He's got the whole world in His hands.
He's got the whole world in His hands.
He's got the whole world in His hands.

Capo loves the sounds
that trains make!

CHUGA, CHUGA
CHOO CHOO!!

Trains move along the tracks...
...and whistle loud and clear.

TOOT!! TOOT!!!

The steam from the engines hisses when they stop...

Hissssss!!!!

Hissssss!!!!

...and when it's time to go again,
the captain shouts out loud:

"All Aboard!!!"

I've Been Working on the Railroad

I've been working on the railroad,

All the live long day.

I've been working on the railroad,

Just to pass the time away.

Can't you hear the whistle blowing?

Rise up so early in the morn.

Can't you hear the captain shouting?

"Dinah blow your horn!"

Dinah won't you blow,

Dinah won't you blow,

Dinah won't you blow your ho-o-orn?

Dinah won't you blow,

Dinah won't you blow,

Dinah won't you blow your horn?

Someone's in the kitchen with Dinah.

Someone's in the kitchen I kno-o-o-ow.

Someone's in the kitchen with Dinah,

Strummin' on the old banjo.

And singin' fee-fi-fidlee-i-o.

Fee-fi-fidlee-i-o-o-o-o.

Fee-fi-fidlee-i-

ooooo ooooo

Strummin' on the old banjo.

Capo is singing and fishing, while the fish swim under the water.

Now Capo is dancing around...

...and singing a little bit louder...

"Hellooo!" says a fish to Capo.
"You sing such a wonderful song!"

"It's fun to sing," says Capo.
"Will you join me in singing along?"

21

Crawdad Song

You get a line, I'll get a pole, Honey.
You get a line, I'll get a pole, Babe.
You get a line, I'll get a pole.
We'll go down to that crawdad hole.
Honey, oh Baby, mine.

Play guitar and sing a song, Honey.
Play guitar and sing a song, Babe.
Play guitar and sing a song.
We'll make music all day long.
Honey, oh Baby, mine.

Let's go walking down the street, Honey.
Let's go walking down the street, Babe.
Let's go walking down the street.
See how many friends we can meet.
Honey, oh Baby, mine.

Let's go over to Jenny's house, Honey.
Let's go over to Jenny's house, Babe.
Let's go over to Jenny's house.
Grab your coat and we'll head on out.
Honey, oh Baby, mine.

1 2 3

BREAKFAST

LUNCH

DINNER

24

CRAWL

WALK

RUN

ABC FUN!

Q Q R R S S

T U V V

W W X X

Y Y and Z Z

Now I know my ABCs
Next time won't you
sing with me?

"What is a Capo?" wonders the Star.

"What is a Star?" wonders Capo.

"Goodnight, Capo."

"Goodnight, Star."

"Can we sing one more song before bedtime?" asks Capo.

"Hmm... OK. Let's twinkle some more," says the Star.

ZZZZzz Zzz Zzzz ZZzzz

Twinkle Twinkle Twinkle Twinkle

...like a diamond in the sky.

Twinkle, twinkle, little star...
How I wonder what you are!

iPlayMusic®

Play Music Together
BEGINNER GUITAR LESSONS: BASICS

How to Use the Book, DVD, and iPod Videos

The book and DVD are designed to be used together. Both have entertaining sections for younger children as well as instructional sections for learning to play guitar. To watch the entertaining segments on the DVD, select "Look ma, no hands!" from the "Play All Songs" category on the left side of the DVD main menu. For instructional sections in the book where we have included videos, you should read through that section and any prior sections before watching the videos. There are four lesson categories on the DVD listed along the right side of the main DVD menu:

> **Guitar Basics**: includes individual lesson videos that go along with the book as you read
> **Song Lessons**: videos that walk you step-by-step through how to play the songs
> **Chord Lessons**: lessons for each chord you'll need to know to play the songs on the DVD
> **Play Individual Songs**: play-along videos for each song that include scrolling chords and lyrics

The DVD has two sides. The side labeled "DVD Video" contains the DVD video, which is playable on any standard DVD player. The side labeled "iPod Videos" contains the iPod videos in a folder called "Drag to iTunes."

Playing the DVD. To play the DVD, simply insert the DVD, with the "DVD Video" side up, into any standard DVD player. If the DVD does not play automatically, then you may have inserted the disk on the wrong side. In this case simply eject the disk, flip it over, and re-insert the DVD.

Exporting the iPod videos. These specially formatted videos are designed for use with your video iPod. Once exported to your iPod, you will have access to all the video lessons and songs, so you can learn and play anytime, anywhere! We recommend that you set your video iPod next to your book, so you can have the videos readily accessible as you read. To export the iPod videos to your video iPod, follow these six steps:

1. Insert the DVD, with the "iPod Videos" side up, into your computer's DVD drive. If your DVD player software launches, then you may have inserted the disk on the wrong side. In this case simply quit the DVD player software, eject the disk, flip it over, and re-insert the DVD.

2. Open the disk by double-clicking. If you are using a Macintosh computer, double-click the "Play Music Together" DVD icon on your desktop to open it. If you are using a Windows computer, go to "My Computer," find your DVD-Rom drive, and double-click it to open it.

3. Launch iTunes.

4. Create a playlist in iTunes.

5. Drag and drop the folder called "Drag to iTunes" from the DVD into the playlist you created in iTunes. All of the videos will now copy to this playlist.

6. Drag and drop the playlist onto your video iPod.

Before we get into the lessons, it is important to understand some basic terminology and the layout of your guitar.

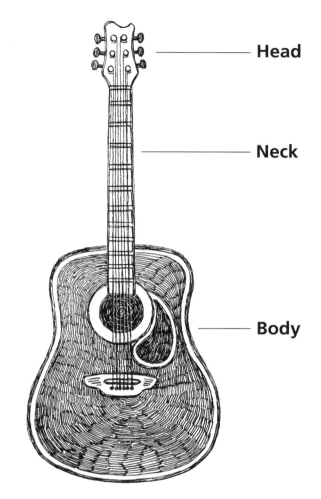

Head

Neck

Body

Figure 1

Guitar Neck

This is the long part of the guitar that the strings run across. The front of the neck is called the **fretboard**.

Guitar Body

This is the largest part of the guitar. Guitar bodies have many different shapes, sizes, and wood types that create a variety of tones. If you have an **acoustic guitar** or *hollow body* **electric guitar**, then it's the part that is hollowed out. If you have an **electric guitar** with a *solid body*, the sound is converted to an electric signal through your guitar pickups that are located under the strings on the body of the guitar. The signal is sent to your amplifier via the guitar cable, and the amplifier then boosts the signal and adds its own character to the sound.

Guitar Anatomy

Guitar Frets

Guitar frets are the **metal strips** on the fretboard of the guitar neck. Frets are spaced apart from each other and span all the way up the neck. Frets exist so that when you press down on a string at a particular position of the neck, the string makes a specific tone. **The higher up** the neck you go, the higher the "pitch" of the sound will be.

VIDEO: *watch Basics Video "Guitar Anatomy"*

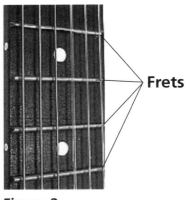

Figure 2

Fret and String Numbering

In this book and in the accompanying videos, we number the frets and strings for simplicity.

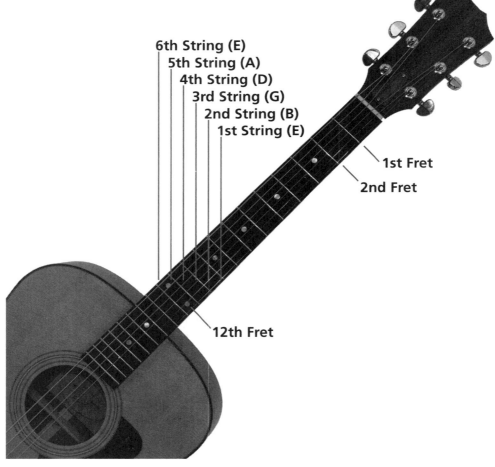

6th String (E)
5th String (A)
4th String (D)
3rd String (G)
2nd String (B)
1st String (E)

1st Fret

2nd Fret

12th Fret

Figure 3

Tuning Keys

There are six tuning keys on the head of your guitar. By turning these keys, you can adjust the tension of the strings on the guitar. By tightening, you can raise the pitch of a particular string. By loosening, you can lower the pitch.

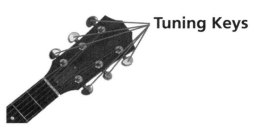

Tuning Keys

Figure 4

Guitar Bridge

The bridge is located at the base of the guitar body. It holds the end of the strings to the guitar on the body.

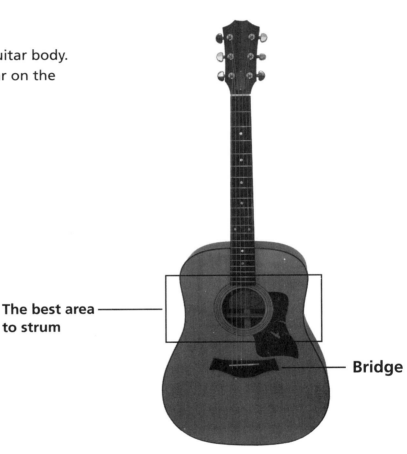

The best area to strum

Bridge

Figure 5

For the best (most resonant) tone, the strings of the guitar should be strummed in-between the base of the neck of the guitar and the bridge of the guitar (the boxed area in figure 5).

These are the essential parts of the guitar that we will be discussing in this book. There is a lot of other guitar-specific and musical terminology that we've chosen to omit, because we want to keep things as simple and straightforward as possible so you can start having fun and playing right away.

Body Positioning

First, find a comfortable place to sit where you can have your legs in front of you and your feet on the ground. This is your **"foundation"** that the guitar will rest on.

Next, make sure you're sitting comfortably and have good posture.

Guitar body resting on right thigh

Feet on the ground

Figure 6

Playing guitar for hours will eventually strain your back if you do not maintain a nice **upright** sitting posture. Pick up your guitar and place the back of the guitar against your stomach. If you are **right-handed**, the guitar neck should be pointing towards your left. Rest the guitar body on your right thigh.

Now place your left hand around the guitar neck and place your right arm around the body so that your hand is lying by the strings. Adjust your body positioning as necessary, so that you are completely comfortable.

Hand Positioning

If you're **left-handed**, don't worry, Jimi Hendrix was left-handed! You basically have two options here. The first option is to buy a right-handed guitar and re-string it, so that the order of the strings in figure 3 is reversed. The second option you have is to buy a left-handed guitar.

If you're **right-handed**, you will use your left hand, as shown below, to construct chords.

As you can see in figure 7, the left-hand fingers are bent and pressing down on the strings on the fretboard. The back of the neck is curved, so that your hand molds into the shape of the neck. In this image, the thumb is arching over the top of the neck. This is a common thumb position for constructing chords.

Figure 7

It is also OK to **press your thumb** into the back of the guitar neck when constructing chords, although this is more common when playing scales. Try both thumb positions and use the one that is most comfortable for you.

Don't worry about what strings your left-hand fingers are pressing down on at this point. We are just trying to get you familiar with the hand and finger positioning.

Figure 8

For the chords you will learn in this section it is very important that you have only your fingertips touching the strings. If any other part of your fingers are touching the strings when you construct a chord, it will sound muffled or muted. **To be clear**, there are many instances, such as when constructing barre chords, that it is perfectly fine, in fact desirable, to allow your entire finger to lay across the strings. However, **for the basic chords** in this lesson, it is important to only press down on the strings with your fingertips.

Right Hand/Arm

This is the hand that you will use to **"strum"** the strings to make the different chord sounds. Remember to position your hand so that when you strike the strings, you are strumming in-between the base of the neck of the guitar and the bridge of the guitar. Remember the boxed area of figure 5 on page 37? This is the most resonant sounding part of the guitar.

Figure 9

Bring your right arm over the guitar. Your **right bicep** should be resting on the top of the body of the guitar. Your **hand** should be positioned directly above the soundhole in the guitar. This is where the sound is produced. Figure 9 shows the correct right-hand/arm positioning.

VIDEO: *watch Basics Video "How to Hold Your Guitar"*

Guitar Pick

The guitar pick is used with the strumming hand to either pick the strings individually or strum them all at once to play chords. Picks come in many shapes and sizes. **The thickness** of the pick is usually marked on the pick. Thickness ranges from thin to heavy. Medium is a good thickness to start with, but you should try a few different gauges and see what thickness you like.

Not all guitarists use a pick. Mark Knopfler, the guitarist from Dire Straits, is perhaps the most famous lead guitarist in the pop music world to use his fingers, rather than a pick, when soloing. Classical, folk, and flamenco guitarists also use fingerstyle rather than a pick to play the guitar. For the most part, it is easier for beginners to produce a nice smooth sound with the pick, so we suggest that you learn how to play with a pick first and then venture off into the world of fingerstyle once you are more advanced.

The guitar pick **is held** with the thumb and index finger of the strumming hand. Grip the fat end of the pick between your thumb and index finger. The pointed part of the pick should be facing in towards the strings. See figure 10.

Striking the strings with the pick

Now that you understand how to hold the pick, you should practice striking individual strings on the guitar. Make sure that you have a firm grip, and then strike the 6th string, making sure that you strike the string with the very **tip** of the pick (about 1/4 of the pick's surface area). In general, if you strike the strings with the same intensity, **the more tip** you have exposed the louder the chord will be. Try striking the 6th string lightly and then more firmly to notice the different tones you can generate. **Avoid** striking the string so hard that it buzzes. This is a sure sign that you're picking too hard.

Figure 10

Figure 11 illustrates how we number each finger when explaining which fingers to place on the fretboard when playing notes and constructing chords.

Figure 11

VIDEO: *watch Basics Video "Finger and String Numbering"*
        watch Basics Video "Making Sound"

Tuning the guitar is **critical**, because nothing you play will sound "right" if the guitar is not in tune. If your guitar is out of tune or tuned incorrectly it will make a perfectly constructed chord sound bad.

There are **many ways** to tune your guitar:

1. With an electronic tuner
2. With tuning software
3. By ear with a tuning fork
4. By ear with another guitar or reference note

The easiest and most accurate way to tune your guitar is with an **electronic tuner** or with tuning software. Electronic tuners typically work for both acoustic or electric guitars, although this is not always the case. An acoustic guitar tuner will have a built-in microphone, to pick up the sound. Electric guitar tuners usually have a 1/4" instrument cable input for the guitar. Most tuners have both a built-in microphone and a 1/4" instrument cable input. We highly recommend that you purchase an electronic tuner, such as the Boss TU-15 Chromatic Tuner.

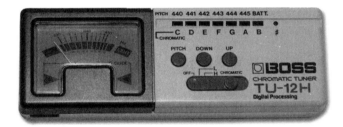

Figure 12

There is also some great free or inexpensive software available for tuning the guitar. Most software tuning products range in cost from $10 to $20 and work with standard computer sound cards and microphones.

Although electronic tuners and software tuners are great tools, we suggest that you learn to tune your guitar by ear to a reference note. **This will help** you to train your ear, so you can quickly tune during a live performance or when you don't have an electronic tuner nearby.

You can also try tuning with a **tuning fork**. A tuning fork will provide you with a reference tone. You can purchase tuning forks at any musical instrument retailer. The most common tuning fork for guitarists generates an A (440) **reference tone**, so you can tune the 5th string (A). In order to generate a tone with the tuning fork, you should lightly tap it against a hard surface and then press the non-forked end against the body of your guitar. This will cause the tone to resonate throughout the guitar body, so that it is louder.

Tuning Your Guitar

Tune your 5th string to the A tuning fork's tone by picking the "open" 5th (A) string ("open" means that you just play the string without pressing down on any frets) while listening to the tone of the tuning fork. **Adjust the tuning key** for your 5th string by turning it in either direction until the tone of the picked string and the tuning fork are identical.

Once your 5th string is in tune, you can tune all the rest of the strings on your guitar. Start with the 6th (E) string. This is the fattest string of the six. It's also the string at the top of the guitar (see figure 3 on page 36, for reference).

Press your index finger on the 5th fret, 6th string. **Make sure** that you press firmly and that your index finger is close to the edge of the fret, almost touching it. If your string is buzzing as you pick it, then either you are not pressing firmly enough, or your finger is not positioned close enough to the edge of the fret.

Pick the 6th string with your index finger pressing down on the 5th fret, 6th string and then pick the "open" 5th (A) string. Compare the two tones. The pitch of the 5th fret, 6th string should be the same sound as the open 5th (A) string. If it is not the exact same sound, turn the 6th string's tuning key so that the sound is the same. Now your 6th and 5th strings are tuned.

Repeat this step, but this time place your index finger on the 5th fret of the 5th string. Pick that string and then pick the open 4th string. They should sound the same. If they don't, turn the tuning key for the 4th string so that the 4th string sounds like the 5th. Be careful to turn the correct tuning key.

Continue the same process from the 4th string to the 3rd string. When you get to tuning the 2nd string there is a slight change. To tune the 2nd (B) string, place your index finger on the 4th fret, 3rd string (instead of the 5th fret). Now pick the 3rd string and then pick the 2nd string. If the 2nd string does not sound like the 3rd, turn the 2nd string's tuning key so that the 2nd string sounds like the 3rd.

Finally, for the 1st (E) string, move your index finger back to the 5th fret on the 2nd string. Then pick the 2nd and 1st strings. The open 1st string should sound exactly like the 5th fret, 2nd string. If it doesn't, then turn the 1st string's tuning key so that it sounds like the 2nd string.

Okay, that is probably going to be the toughest part of learning to play guitar. We recommend you buy an electronic tuner, but knowing how to tune the guitar by ear will be extremely valuable, especially in live playing situations or at times when you don't have access to a tuner.

VIDEO: *watch Basics Video "Tuning Your Guitar"*
      watch Basics Video "Practice Playing Strings"

Now for the fun stuff. In this section we will teach you the basic chords you need to know to play the songs you love. So let's get started!

Before we move on to chord construction, here are some basic tips that will help you sound better.

1. Press firmly

Be sure you press each finger down so that it firmly presses the string against the fretboard. This will ensure the sound of the string is clean and does not buzz. If you don't push the string down hard enough you will hear a buzzing or a muffled sound.

2. Close to the fret

In general (this is not always the case), make sure that your finger is as close to the fret as possible without actually touching the fret. This will ensure that the string does not buzz or sound muffled when played.

3. One finger per string

Be sure that only one finger touches each string. Oftentimes you will find one finger slightly touching a neighboring string. This is particularly common with the more difficult chords (like the G Major chord). This is one other cause of muffled or buzzing strings. Take some time after constructing the chord to make sure that each finger is only touching the necessary strings and not resting on neighboring strings.

4. Relax

Relax your hand so that it is comfortable when constructing the chord. Re-position your wrist for each chord so that you are comfortable and so that your fingers can sustain their position (without cramping) while you strum.

On the following pages you will find pictures and **videos** (contained on the DVD) that explain the finger placement for five chords: C Major, G Major, A Major, D Major, and F Major. These five chords are used in the songs on the DVD and are some of the most widely used chords in popular songs today.

By learning to play **just these five chords** you will know the building blocks of many popular songs by some of the biggest recording artists.

Look at each chord diagram closely. Spend some time positioning your fingers to look like the images. Try constructing these chords yourself, strumming them, and listening to how they sound.

If you are having trouble, don't panic. Just play the **chord videos** from the Chord Lessons section on the DVD to watch the instructor construct the chords step by step.

VIDEO: *watch Basics Video "Constructing Chords"*

Basic Chords

C Major

VIDEO: *watch Chord Lessons Video "C Major Chord"*

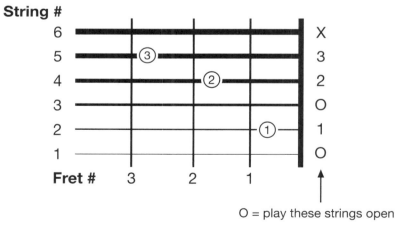

O = play these strings open
X = do not play these strings

G Major

VIDEO: *watch Chord Lessons Video "G Major Chord"*

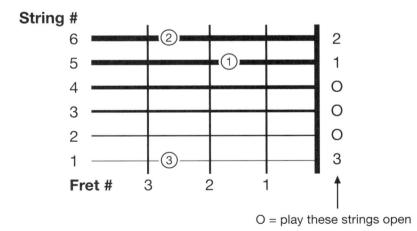

O = play these strings open

Basic Chords

A Major

VIDEO: *watch Chord Lessons Video "A Major Chord"*

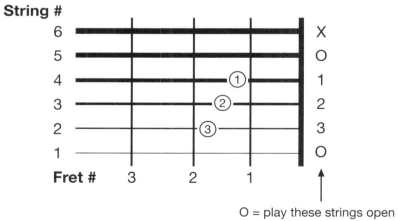

O = play these strings open
X = do not play these strings

D Major

VIDEO: *watch Chord Lessons Video "D Major Chord"*

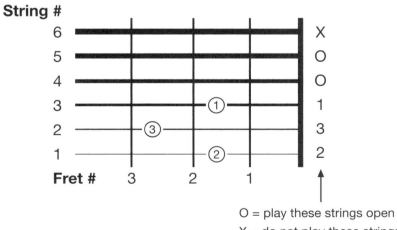

O = play these strings open
X = do not play these strings

F Major

VIDEO: *watch Chord Lessons Video "F Major Chord"*

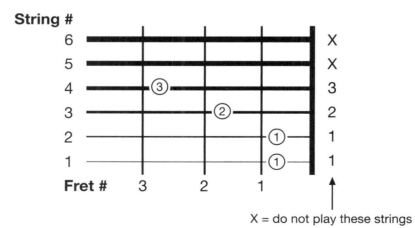

X = do not play these strings

Now that you are comfortable with five chords, it's time to start making music. There are **three fundamentals** you will need in order to play songs:

1. **Chord construction (which we just covered)**

2. **Strumming patterns**

3. **Transitions**

Knowing the chords is the first step in playing music. If you're right-handed, you use your **left hand** to construct chords and your **right hand** to strum the guitar. When you strum chords, you play the strings of your guitar with your picking hand either with a downstroke or an upstroke. **Strumming patterns** are combinations of down- and upstrokes that make rhythmic sense. Here are the **basic rules** to remember when strumming the guitar:

1. Don't break your wrist. When strumming the guitar, over 90% of the motion in your right arm should be in twisting your forearm, not breaking your wrist. Your wrist should remain firm and not flimsy. If your wrist is flimsy, your strumming will sound sloppy. Most of the up-down motion of your hand should be controlled by turning your entire forearm. Use your elbow to help your forearm move up and down.

2. Maintain a firm grip on the pick. Make sure that you grasp the pick firmly, or else you will not be able to generate a nice tone from the guitar. Refer back to page 40 for a refresher on proper pick technique.

3. Your arm is a windshield wiper. Visually, you should think of your arm as a windshield wiper that is moving up and down at the same pace, over and over. Don't ever stop your arm from moving up and down. Keep a nice rhythm. The key is to only play the up- and downstrokes when you want to generate sound, but to always keep your arm moving up and down at a constant and steady rhythm, just like a windshield wiper.

In this section you will learn how to play one popular strumming pattern.

A **strumming pattern** consists of downstrokes and upstrokes.

A **downstroke** is played by strumming the guitar strings from the top of the guitar to the bottom – or from the 6th (low E) string to the 1st (high E) string. We will represent a downstroke with a down arrow:

Strumming Patterns

An **upstroke** is played by strumming the guitar strings from the bottom of the guitar to the top – or from the 1st (high E) string to the 6th (low E) string. We will represent an upstroke with an up arrow:

Remember to think of your strumming hand as a windshield wiper, or a pendulum. **A dashed arrow** will represent the direction your arm should be moving as you swing your arm up and down without hitting the strings.

If you need further instruction, or these concepts seem a bit confusing, please watch the "Strumming Basics" video.

VIDEO: *watch Basics Video "Strumming Basics"*

With just the following **strumming pattern** you will have the ability to play many popular songs.

Let's get started.

Strumming pattern: Down, down, up, down, down, up.

Try this strumming pattern with any of the five chords you've already learned.

If you need further instruction on this strumming pattern, please watch the video for an explanation from the instructor.

Now you know how to play a strumming pattern with just one chord. The next step is to play this strumming pattern while transitioning **between chords**.

The most important thing to remember when learning how to transition between chords is to start out SLOWLY.

Try playing a few downstrokes with the D chord and then switch to the G chord. Try to keep your strumming arm moving at a constant rhythm as you transition between chords. Slow down as much as you need to in order to ensure that your strumming arm never skips a beat. Even if it feels painfully slow, this is the only way to become proficient at changing between chords.

Another very important thing to remember is to keep your strumming arm moving at a constant, steady motion, just like a windshield wiper. You'll be amazed at how quickly you can increase the speed (or tempo) of your strumming arm if you start slowly and build up.

The trick to making transitions sound smooth is to play some open high strings or muted strings as you make your transition from one chord to another. **This ensures** that you maintain the rhythmic sound of the strumming pattern as you transition between chords. For a more in-depth explanation of this transition trick, **watch the videos** on the DVD to learn from the instructor.

VIDEO: *watch Basics Video "Practice Drill"*

It's important to work on keeping rhythm and tempo as you play strumming patterns and transition between chords. Remember to start slowly. Don't try to go really fast until you are totally comfortable at a slower tempo. Work your way up to a comfortable speed. You'll soon find that with just a little practice you'll be playing at any speed you want with any chords and strumming patterns. Eventually you'll even start coming up with your own patterns!

Practice Tips

There are two important things to remember when you practice your guitar:

1. Start slowly

Remember not to rush when you learn something new. It is always tempting to try to start playing a new chord or strumming pattern at full speed, because you are excited and want to hear it the way it is supposed to sound. If you slow down and spend an hour or so nailing the chord construction, strumming pattern, and transitions, you will have that song under your belt for the rest of your life. Conversely, if you try to play it at full speed right away and get frustrated, you may never learn it.

2. Play with a metronome

If possible, always have a metronome with you when you practice. A metronome is a device that plays a "click" sound to the tempo (or speed) that you specify. Practice your transitions and strumming patterns to the beat of a metronome. That way you will develop some discipline around maintaining the "windshield wiper" rhythm with your strumming arm. Set the metronome to a slow tempo at first and then gradually increase the tempo until you are up to speed.

If you remember these two important rules, you will have **productive practice sessions**, and you'll be playing like a pro sooner than you can imagine.

This approach may seem slow and methodical, but it is **amazing how quickly** you can get up to speed if you start slowly. It is an exponential increase – suddenly, one day you can play fast. It seems to happen overnight!

Your **fingers** are going to hurt when you first start playing. This is actually a good sign, and eventually you will develop calluses that keep the tips of your fingers protected. This can take a little time, but we recommend playing until your fingers start to get uncomfortable. When this happens take a break. There is no need to overstimulate your fingertips, so just take your time. The pain will go away and you will eventually find that you will be able to play for longer and longer periods of time with no pain at all.

Your **hands**, especially the hand you use to construct chords, may also get sore. This is very normal, and you should make sure to take plenty of breaks as you practice so that you give your hand time to rest. Eventually you will build hand strength. Remember to set a time every day for practice, even if it's only 15 minutes. This is enough time to develop **"muscle memory."** Eventually your hands will just know what to do. It's a strange phenomenon, but the more you practice, the more you start remembering with your hands instead of your brain. When you get to this point, playing becomes really fun!

iPlayMusic ®

Play Music Together
Lyrics with Chords

If You're Happy and You Know It

      D   A
If you're happy and you know it, clap your hands (clap clap).

     A   D
If you're happy and you know it, clap your hands (clap clap).

      G   D
If you're happy and you know it and you really want to show it,

     A   D
If you're happy and you know it, clap your hands (clap clap).

      D   A
If you're happy and you know it, stomp your feet (stomp stomp).

     A   D
If you're happy and you know it, stomp your feet (stomp stomp).

      G   D
If you're happy and you know it and you really want to show it,

     A   D
If you're happy and you know it, stomp your feet (stomp stomp).

      D   A
If you're happy and you know it, shout "hooray!" (hoo-ray).

     A   D
If you're happy and you know it, shout "hooray!" (hoo-ray).

      G   D
If you're happy and you know it and you really want to show it,

     A   D
If you're happy and you know it, shout "hooray!" (hoo-ray).

      D   A
If you're happy and you know it, do all three (clap clap, stomp stomp, hoo-ray!).

     A   D
If you're happy and you know it, do all three (clap clap, stomp stomp, hoo-ray!).

      G   D
If you're happy and you know it and you really want to show it,

     A   D
If you're happy and you know it, do all three (clap clap, stomp stomp, hoo-ray!).

The Wheels on the Bus

C   G   C
The wheels on the bus go round and round, round and round, round and round.

C   G   C
The wheels on the bus go round and round, all through the town.

C   G   C
The wipers on the bus go swish, swish, swish, swish, swish, swish, swish, swish, swish.

C   G   C
The wipers on the bus go swish, swish, swish, all through the town.

C   G   C
The horn on the bus goes beep, beep, beep, beep, beep, beep, beep, beep, beep.

C   G   C
The horn on the bus goes beep, beep, beep, all through the town.

C   G   C
The money on the bus goes clink, clink, clink, clink, clink, clink, clink, clink, clink.

C   G   C
The money on the bus goes clink, clink, clink, all through the town.

C   G   C
The babies on the bus go wah, wah, wah, wah, wah, wah, wah, wah, wah.

C   G   C
The babies on the bus go wah, wah, wah, all through the town.

C   G   C
The mommy on the bus goes shh, shh, shh, shh, shh, shh, shh, shh, shh.

C   G   C
The mommy on the bus goes shh, shh, shh, all through the town.

C   G   C
The wheels on the bus go round and round, round and round, round and round.

C   G   C
The wheels on the bus go round and round, all through the town.

He's Got The Whole World in His Hands

             C
He's got the whole world in His hands.

             G
He's got the whole world in His hands.

             C
He's got the whole world in His hands.

             G   C
He's got the whole world in His hands.

             C
He's got the wind and the rain in His hands.

             G
He's got the wind and the rain in His hands.

             C
He's got the wind and the rain in His hands.

             G   C
He's got the whole world in His hands.

             C
He's got the little bitty baby in His hands.

             G
He's got the little bitty baby in His hands.

             C
He's got the little bitty baby in His hands.

             G   C
He's got the whole world in His hands.

             C
He's got the whole world in His hands.

             G
He's got the whole world in His hands.

             C
He's got the whole world in His hands.

             G   C
He's got the whole world in His hands.

I've Been Working on the Railroad

D   G   D
I've been working on the railroad, all the live long day.

D   A
I've been working on the railroad, just to pass the time away.

A   D   G   D
Can't you hear the whistle blowing? Rise up so early in the morn.

G   D   A   D
Can't you hear the captain shouting? "Dinah blow your horn!"

D   G   A   D
Dinah won't you blow, Dinah won't you blow, Dinah won't you blow your ho-o-orn?

D   G   A   D
Dinah won't you blow, Dinah won't you blow, Dinah won't you blow your horn?

D   D   A
Someone's in the kitchen with Dinah. Someone's in the kitchen I kno-o-o-ow.

D   G   D   A   D
Someone's in the kitchen with Dinah, strummin' on the old banjo and singin'...

D   D   A
Fee-fi-fidlee-i-o. Fee-fi-fidlee-i-o-o-o-o.

D   G   D   A   D
Fee-fi-fidlee-i-o, strummin' on the old banjo.

D   D   A
Fee-fi-fidlee-i-o. Fee-fi-fidlee-i-o-o-o-o.

D   G
Fee-fi-fidlee-i-ooooooo...

D   A   D
Strummin' on the old banjo!

Crawdad Song

C   C   G
You get a line, I'll get a pole, Honey. You get a line, I'll get a pole, Babe.
C   F   C   G   C
You get a line, I'll get a pole. We'll go down to that crawdad hole. Honey, oh Baby, mine.

C   C   G
Play guitar and sing a song, Honey. Play guitar and sing a song, Babe.
C   F   C   G   C
Play guitar and sing this song. We'll make music all day long. Honey, oh Baby, mine.

C   C   G
Let's go walking down the street, Honey. Let's go walking down the street, Babe.
C   F   C   G   C
Let's go walking down the street. See how many friends we can meet. Honey, oh Baby, mine.

C   C   G
Let's go over to Jenny's house, Honey. Let's go over to Jenny's house, Babe.
C   F   C   G   C
Let's go over to Jenny's house. Grab your coat and we'll head on out. Honey, oh Baby, mine.

C   C   G
You get a line, I'll get a pole, Honey. You get a line, I'll get a pole, Babe.
C   F   C   G   C
You get a line, I'll get a pole. We'll go down to that crawdad hole. Honey, oh Baby, mine.

C   G   C
Honey, oh Baby, mine.
C   G   C
Honey, oh Baby, mine.

ABC Song

C   F   C

A, B, C, D, E, F, G,

F   C   G   C

H, I, J, K, L, M, N, O, P,

C   F

Q, R, S,

C   G

T, U, V,

C F

W, X,

C   G

Y and Z.

C   F C

Now I know my ABCs

F   C   G   C

Next time won't you sing with me?

Twinkle, Twinkle, Little Star

C   F   C
Twinkle, twinkle, little star,

F   C   G   C
How I wonder what you are.

C   F   C   G
Up above the world so high,

C   F   C   G
Like a diamond in the sky.

C   F   C
Twinkle, twinkle, little star,

F   C   G   C
How I wonder what you are!

Next Steps

We hope you have enjoyed **Play Music Together** and that you will come visit us at our website: **www.iPlayMusic.com**

We are constantly developing new innovative products that deliver the unique joy and experience of making music. Stay tuned for many more exciting products to come!

Thank you for purchasing **Play Music Together** from iPlayMusic. On behalf of the entire iPlayMusic team, we wish you success in your newfound passion! We would love to hear from you and value **your feedback**. Please send us your comments and any ideas you might have for additional instructional tools and videos: **feedback@iplaymusic.com**

Other Products by iPlayMusic

iPlayMusic offers books, DVDs, software, musical instruments and accessories - everything the aspiring musician needs to learn, play, create and share music! **If you liked Play Music Together**, then we recommend the following products, available today at www.iPlayMusic.com:

Beginner Guitar Lessons Level 1 Book and DVD
Perfect for beginners of all ages, the award-winning iPlayMusic method is the most fun, simple, and easy way to learn and enjoy guitar. The Level 1 book and DVD combination teaches you to play quickly and easily without complex music notation or theory. This product includes a 64-page book, over 2 hours of video lessons, and 5 popular song lessons.

Beginner Guitar Lessons Level 2 DVD
Take your guitar playing to the next level and learn new songs and styles. iPlayMusic Beginner Guitar Lessons Level 2 teaches you new riffs, licks and techniques, and then how to play four new songs right away. Level 2 features rock, blues and country / western songs and also introduces you to reggae and the 12-bar blues.

Beginner Guitar Lessons Mac and Windows Software
Learn to play hit songs from artists like the Beatles, Eric Clapton, Johnny Cash and Bob Marley! Play 26 hit songs, including classics like "Yellow Submarine," "I Shot the Sheriff," and "Redemption Song." iPlayMusic lessons are created for both Macintosh and Windows. Export and view lessons on the video iPod and create, record, and share your own version of the song with professional music creation software and backing tracks (included). There is no more fun and easy way to make music!

The vision of iPlayMusic, Inc. is to deliver the unique joy and experience of making music to novice and non-musicians. In **Play Music Together** we present colorful stories and illustrations, kids songs, entertaining video segments, and comprehensive beginner guitar instruction - a complete package for the entire family to play and sing together.

iPlayMusic, Inc. was formed by a group of friends with 20 years of combined playing and teaching experience. The award-winning iPlayMusic® teaching method has gained critical acclaim among reviewers, industry experts, and seasoned musicians. Our teaching method has been refined over the years through conversations with customers, friends, instructors, advanced players, and absolute beginners. Based on this research, we decided early on to focus on teaching people the skills they need to play songs as soon as possible. We hope you have picked up skills from this product that help you experience the joy of playing songs on guitar!

Sincerely,

The iPlayMusic Team
Quincy
Jen
Noel
Rich
Chris
Mike

Index